P9-CBH-747

GREEK MUSIC, VERSE AND DANCE

Da Capo Press Music Reprint Series

GREEK MUSIC, VERSE AND DANCE

By Thrasybulos Georgiades

Translated from the German by
Erwin Benedikt and Marie Louis Martinez

DA CAPO PRESS · NEW YORK · 1973

Library of Congress Cataloging in Publication Data

Georgiades, Thrasybulos Georgos, 1907-
   Greek music, verse, and dance.

   (Da Capo Press music reprint series)
   Translation of Der griechische Rhythmus.
   Reprint of the ed. published by Merlin Press, New
York, which was issued as v. 5 of Merlin music books.
   1. Music, Greek and Roman. 2. Greek language—
Metrics and rhythmics. I. Title.
[ML169.G373   1973]   700'.938   73-4336
ISBN 0-306-70561-3

This Da Capo Press edition of
Greek Music, Verse and Dance
is an unabridged republication of the 1955
edition published in New York.

Published by Da Capo Press, Inc.
A Subsidiary of Plenum Publishing Corporation
227 West 17th Street, New York, N.Y. 10011

Manufactured in the United States of America

GREEK MUSIC,

VERSE and DANCE

GREEK MUSIC,

VERSE and DANCE

THRASYBULOS GEORGIADES

Translated from the German by
Erwin Benedikt and Marie Louise Martinez

MERLIN PRESS - NEW YORK

Printed in Germany

CONTENTS

ΜΙΔΑΙ ΑΥΛΗΤΗΙ ΑΚΡΑΓΑΝΤΙΝΩΙ

Αιτεω σε, φιλαγ λαε, καλλιστα βροτεαν πολιων,
Φερσεφονας εδος α τ' οχθαις επι μηλοβοτου
ναιεις Ακραγαντος ευδ ματον κολωναν, ω ανα,
ιλαος αθανατων ανδρων τε συν ευμενια
δεξαι στεφανωμα τοδ εκ Πυθωνος ευδοξω Μιδα
αυτον τε νιν Ελλαδα νικασαντα τεχ'να, ταν ποτε
Παλλας εφευρε θρασειαν < Γοργονων >
ουλιον θρηνον διαπ'λεξαισ' 'Αθανα.

τον παρθενιοις υπο τ' απ'λατοις οφιων κεφαλαις
αιε λειβομενον δυσπενθει συν καματω,
Περσευς οποτε τ'ριτον αυσεν κασιγ'νηταν μερος
ενναλια Σεριφω λαοισι τε μοιραν αγων.
ητοι το τε θεσπεσιον Φορκοι' αμαυρωσεν γενος,
λυγ'ρον τ' ερανον Πολυδεκτα θηκε ματροσ τ' εμπεδον
δουλοσυναν το τ' αναγκαιον λεχος,
ευπαραου κρατα συλαις Μεδοισας

υιος Δαναας. τον απο χ'ρυσου φαμεν αυτορυτου
εμμεναι. αλλ' επει εκ τουτων φιλον ανδρα πονων
ερρυσατο, παρθενος αυλων τευχε παμφωνον μελος,

οφ'ρα τον Ευρυαλας εκ καρπαλιμαν γεννων
χριμφθεντα συν εντεσι μιμησαιτ' ερικ'λαγκταν γοον.
ευρεν θεος. αλλα νιν ευροισ' ανδρασι θ'νατοις εχειν,
ωνυμασεν κεφαλαν πολλαν νομον,
ευκλεα λαοσσοων μναστηρ' αγωνων,

λεπτου διανισομενον χαλκου θαμα και δονακων,
τοι παρα καλλιχορω ναιοισι πολι Χαριτων
Καφισιδος εν τεμενει, πιστοι χορευταν μαρτυρες.
ει δε τις ολβος εν ανθρωποισιν, ανευ καματου
ου φαινεται. εκ δε τελευτασει νιν ητοι σαμερον
δαιμων — το δε μορσιμον ουπαρφυκτον —, αλλ' εσται
        χρονος
ουτος, ο και τιν' αελπτια βαλων
εμπαλιν γνωμας το μεν δωσει, το δ' ουπω.

To Midas aulos-player of Akragas

[I] entreat Thee, splendor-loving, fairest [of] mortal
cities,
Persephone's home, that and [the] hilltops on [of
the] sheep-pasturing
dost inhabit Akragas' fair-built crest, oh Queen,
propitiously [of] Immortals and [of] men with
kindliness
receive crown this from Putho [from] well-famed
Midas
him and [him] self [who] Hellas conquered [in the]
art which once
Pallas invented [of the] fierce Gorgons
deathful dirge plaiting, Athena,

which [of the] maidens beneath and [of the] fearful
snakes heads
[she] heard welling forth heaviness of heart with
sorrow
Perseus as [the] third killed [of] the sisters part
[to the] isle Seriphos [to its] folk and doom bringing;
verily that and weird [of] Phorkos bereft of light
progeny
banefully and banquet [to] Polydektes prepared
[to] the mother and continuing
slavery the and enforced bridal couch
[of her] fair-cheeked head refting [the] Medusa,

[the] son [of] Danae, who of gold [we] ever free-
flowing
[to] be. But when from these [the] beloved man toils

redeemed [the] Maiden [of the] shawms [she]
       fashioned many-voiced tune,
in order that [she] Euryales [from] the ravening jaws
gushing with instruments render loud-resounding
       lamentation
devised [it the] Goddess. But it [having] devised,
       [to] men mortal [as a] possession,
[she] named [the] Many Headed Strain,
[the] noble folk-arousing summoner [to] contests,

[the] thin issues bronze often and reeds
which by [of the] gay with dance grow city [of the]
       Graces
Kephisos in precincts, faithful [of the] dancers
       witnesses.
If however any bliss among men, without toil
not showeth [it]; to the full verily [will] accomplish
       [it] now even today
a god, the for Fate [is] not avoidable; but [there]
       will come [that] time,
such [a one] which also [although it] one [with]
       despair smote,
against expectation the one [thing] gives, the other
       not.

GREEK MUSIC,

VERSE and DANCE

I

WE HAVE NO DIRECT ACCESS to Greek music. All our information about it is secondary and has come to us through musico-theoretical works, references of poets and writers, paintings on vases and representations on reliefs. Such knowledge is, however, empty, and dead, since the music itself has vanished forever. We do have firsthand information about Greek verse and poetry. This poetry was not only related to music, but formed an entity with it. The uniting element was

15

Greek rhythm, and this rhythm is known to us through verse. The rhythm of Greek verse was one and the same in poetry and music. In the chorus, which was actually danced, the rhythm of the verse also constituted that of the dance.

The title of our book, *Music, Verse and Dance,* does not mean that we shall consider each of these three concepts separately. Instead, we shall look upon them as a unit, as did the ancients. Today this unit is evident primarily through the rhythm; in reality, however, it had its roots in the particular character and mentality of the Greeks and was inherent in their language. That music, verse and dance should be regarded as a unit is by no means self-evident to us. If we are to understand such a phenomenon we must observe it from various angles. Specifically, we shall return again and again to certain characteristics of

Greek language. Thus we shall concern ourselves with one and the same phenomenon, each time adding new color to it and attempting to extract always something new: the theme of our essay demands, as it were, treatment in variation form. It does not lend itself to a presentation in continuous chronological order proceeding step by step from older to more recent times.

Instead of a general and abstract treatment of our theme, we shall relate it to a concrete example. We shall consider a single chorus which, through content, music, language, verse and dance, will exemplify the meaning of all problems. We have selected the Twelfth Pythian Ode of Pindar (born ca. 520, died after 446), who was active in the first half of the fifth century B.C. and thus was a contemporary of the oldest tragedian, Aeschylus. His work falls into the earliest classical period in which the classical Parthenon, for example, had not yet been built. Pindar wrote choruses, "odes" for celebrations held in honor of the victors of Greek games. Pindar was commissioned by the victors themselves, and these odes were performed — sometimes under Pindar's own supervision — during the festive receptions of the heroes in their homelands. Other than the Olympic Games, the Pythian contests at Delphi were the most famous.

The ode to be discussed was created for a victor in the Pythian contests ca. 490 and belongs to the earliest works of Pindar. (The order in which these odes have come down to us is not chronological. Our ode, Number 12, for instance, appears as the last of the Pythian Odes.) It is one of his shorter and rhythmically rather simple victory odes. The work deals with music, honoring Midas, an aulos player

who has won a contest in the art of aulos
playing. (The aulos, related to the modern
oboe, was the typical wind instrument of
the Greeks.) Midas hailed from Agrigent,
a Greek colony in Sicily. The song begins
with an invocation to that city, which
Pindar imagines to be a real being.
Agrigent is to receive Midas, who was
crowned with a laurel wreath after his
victory in aulos playing over Greece
(Greece in the narrow sense, in contrast
to the colonies). Pindar tells us how this
art was invented by Athena: when
Perseus beheaded Medusa, Athena heard
the mourning of the sisters. After she had
freed Perseus from his toil, she invented
aulos playing in the form of a specific
tune to represent their loud, heartrending cries. She gave this paradigm to
human beings as a noble summoner to the
contests bringing the people together and
called it the "Many-heads-tune" (prob-

ably alluding to the many heads of the snakes of Medusa and her sisters).The tune flows through the thin copper and the reed, the mouthpiece of the aulos; this reed grows near the city of Charites, with its beautiful round dances — in the holy region of Kephisís on Lake Kopais in Boethia; and the same reed, and therewith the aulos, bears true witness to dancing. The ode ends with a retrospective glance, a resume of what has been heard, referring as much to the deed of Perseus and the invention of the aulos by Athena as to the victory of Midas: when good fortune is bestowed upon a man, it does not come without his previous effort. Thus, in accordance with inexorable fate, a daemon had always disposed of fortune's favor, in past and in present; and it will be so in the future when time unexpectedly grants a man, long waiting in vain, one favor but yet not another.

We see that even the content of this chorus touches upon our theme: Pindar describes aulos playing as a divine invention and, specifically, as a representation of loud mourning. Thereby he gives a clearly outlined conception of the origin of music in general. A particular type of music is captured in this legend, and further, it is said that a tune of divine origin becomes the prototype for musical imitations by human beings. This prototype is like the ancestor of a musical species. There is also a description of the instrument, the aulos, which is directly related to dancing. The music — the tune under discussion — is connected with human beings in a twofold manner: as the representation of pain, and as an artistic deed which, though rewarding the effort, is inseparably bound to human destiny in a manner defying all inquiry. The content of the ode comes to us in the form of verses which embody the music and are at the same time realized as dance movement through the chorus. ("Chorus" to the Greeks meant a unity of the singing of the verse and of dancing; only in later times was this designation limited to singing.)

II

*I*NSTEAD OF CONCERNING ourselves at this point with the content or with the unity of music, verse and dance as embodied in the chorus, let us begin with the examination of the rhythm. The underlying principle of Greek rhythm is extremely simple and easy to understand. Use is made of only two time values, two "quantities" (for this reason Greek rhythm is termed "quantitative rhythm"): the "short" and the "long." The symbol of the short is ∪, that of the

long, — . The relationship of the short
to the long is, as a rule, 1 : 2 (∪ — = ♩ ♩).
The long is therefore twice as long as the
short. This holds true for our example,
even though there are other categories of
verse which, as we will see later, are
based on the relationship 1 : 1½ (∪ — =
♩ ♩.). It is through the varying juxta-
positions of longs and shorts that the
verse rhythms originate. In this way
Pindar forms the strophe of our ode,
which consists of eight lines ("periods").
The entire ode consists of four such
strophes so that the rhythmic scheme is
repeated four times.

Let us attempt to reproduce this
rhythm. We receive the impression that
the longs and shorts are placed at random,
that they are simply lined up in a row as
if by chance. As we survey the entire
rhythm we find that certain correspondences exist, that, in fact, certain patterns

are repeated. The following rhythms, in particular, impress themselves upon us: ∪ ∪ — and — ∪ —. We can even assume that the alternation of these patterns was intentional, i. e., as if it originated from the endeavor to blend one pattern into the other. Both patterns end with ∪ — , but they may begin with ∪ or — : ⊽ ∪ — . In this manner the complete strophe originates through the varied repetition of but one rhythmic pattern. Aside from this pattern only single longs are utilized. Thus at the beginning of each of the first seven lines one or two longs precede the pattern ∪ ∪ — ; within the lines one long may be interpolated between the patterns. The last line is conspicuous. All the others contain, aside from single longs, either the first pattern ∪ ∪ — alone or, in addition, the second — ∪ — , and they invariably end with (⊽) ∪ — . But the last line is different. Here we find only the

second pattern, — ∪ — . Still more
peculiar is the fact that the ending does
not consist of ∪ — , for one long is
added to it, resulting in the rhythm
— ∪ — — . The last line is brought about
by the threefold repetition of this
rhythm. This last line thus brings an
inversion, as it were, of the characteristic
pattern. Instead of — ∪ ∪ — or — — ∪ — ,
it presents — ∪ — — . It is the only line
not preceded by a long but followed by
one. In this manner, it develops, as it
were, countermovement by means of
which Pindar brings the entire strophe to
its conclusion, to rest. This countermovement calls to mind the so-called *contrapost*
in the plastic arts of the Greeks, the
contrast between the supporting and the
suspended leg of a statue.

Interpreted in this fashion, the rhythmic construction of this strophe appears
intelligible. Any attempt, however, to find

a repetition of a definite unit of measurement would end in failure because a governing and fixed measurement of time (such as the musical measure as we know it in more recent music) cannot be applied here, if for no other reason than the absence of a definite order of accentuation. Added to this is the fact that the two rhythmic patterns quoted contain a different number of temporal units. If we choose the short as a temporal unit, one of the patterns, ∪ ∪ —— , contains four shorts, whereas the other, —— ∪ —— , contains five. Furthermore, there are the freely added longs. If we were to apply a unit of measurement similar to that of the modern musical measure, it would have to fluctuate inasmuch as it would have to contain four, five or seven temporal units. In other words, it would not serve its purpose, for it would not be a fixed unit of measurement.

We must therefore renounce the attempt to apply a measurement of time containing smaller units and repeating itself continually. Instead, we must proceed from the smallest temporal unit given here, namely, from the short. We can establish only from case to case how many of such temporal units are contained in the rhythmic patterns under consideration. The rhythmic patterns themselves originated solely through the joining of the two given elements, the short and the long. To be sure, the Greeks were guided in this procedure by the need for certain characteristic turns, by the need for repetitions, correspondences, alterations and, of course, by the need for variety. They did not presuppose a larger unit of measurement similar to our musical measure and thus the small rhythmic figures which we should like to compare to small physical bodies, originated. Like physical bodies they have their own clearly defined extension and are of definite dimension. They consist of the two different building stones, the short and the long.

Metrical rhythm is just the opposite. It consists of the repetition of an always identical measure which it takes for granted. This measure, however, is not the same as a definite rhythm, for it remains but a scheme, a general prerequisite for the arrangement of a specific rhythm. The measure has more of the significance of a general law than of a definite rhythm. The actual, the concrete rhythm in the individual case originates through the subdivision of the given musical measure in a definite manner. One can use whole, half, quarter or eighth notes, etc., ad libitum, or one can tie notes over, or introduce syncopations or rests. The important thing is the possibility of the *subdivision* of a given measure, a possibility completely absent from Greek rhythm because the unit of time is the smallest element, the short, and is therefore indivisible. It was called *chronos prōtos,* i. e., "primary time." Rhythm, instead of originating through subdivision, came about through *addition.*

The western temporal unit, on the other hand, is an empty measure which must first be filled with concrete note values. Precisely this fact constitutes the essential difference between ancient and western rhythm.

The principle of the pre-existing, empty unit of measurement which is subdivided rhythmically and filled with concrete note values is valid for the entire western concept of rhythm, including the medieval. It applies to the rhythm of medieval mensural notation; it becomes particularly evident in the measure of classic and romantic music, for here a definite and predetermined order of accentuation is added. In 2/4 time, for example, one takes for granted that the first beat of the measure is accented, the second unaccented; in 3/4 time the first of the three beats receives the accent. A similar principle is applicable to the composite meters. Beyond that, several measures are often combined into a unit; this is true particularly of dance movements or of quick movements such as the scherzo, but it holds true also for song forms. One feels that the second measure of a series is twice as heavy as the first; a similar relationship exists between the fourth and the second measures and between the eighth and the fourth. The result, therefore, is an accumulation of weight in the manner of a dynamic progression: two-four-eight, etc. Of course, this is not the only possible series, there are others such

31

as three-six-twelve, etc. Generally speaking, in such rhythms the principle of multiplication is just as characteristic as that of subdivision; it incorporates, as we have seen, a *dynamic* idea. Within such a rhythm one feels a kind of immanent crescendo with the potential for producing climaxes. This dynamic character has the effect of cementing the various rhythmic values.

All of this is in contrast to Greek rhythm, which originates through simple addition and is loosely put together; the rhythmic principle of the Greeks thereby has a pronounced *static* character. This may be observed in our example: it is impossible to execute the rhythm of the Pindar strophe with the verve of a Beethoven scherzo or a Strauss waltz. Equally, the evenness of measured music, as in Palestrina, for instance, is absent. One is compelled to progress step by step from one small particle to the next. One cannot glide over the rhythm, as it were, but must remain on solid ground — indeed one must adhere fast to it, following each small turn as it presents itself.

This difference between Greek and western rhythm permits of another statement, no less significant. Let us realize how a certain rhythm originates within the province of western rhythm, particularly within the rhythm of the measure: first we determine an absolute law, an abstract order of accentuation, the meter, and only then do we undertake to fill the scheme with concrete rhythmic values. Obviously, this is a dual procedure. We distinguish between the general order of accentuation and the actual length of the individual rhythmic values. Such a distinction does not exist in Greek rhythm, for here time is measured through the concrete rhythmic elements themselves, the short and the long. They are, as we have said before, like two physical bodies with definite dimension. Thus the finished rhythm does not originate in two stages, but all at once and out of nothing, as it were. The distinguishing feature of the western temporal unit is "unfilled-in" time, existing independently of its content, that of the Greek temporal unit is "filled-in" time, in which the time span and its content are identical. This contrast between "unfilled-in" and "filled-in" time leads us to the very core of the rhythmic phenomenon. Once it has been understood, it is impossible to confuse Greek rhythm with that of western civilization.

As a consequence of this principle of "unfilled-in" time, polyphony becomes possible in western music, for since the measure exists as "unfilled-in" time it may be "filled-in" at the same time in different ways in different vocal parts. These individual parts are held together by a common basic unit of time, but this basic unit can be subdivided differently in different parts. As a result, the individual parts in polyphonic music may be distinguished one from another by their own individual rhythms. It is, however, the very nature of Greek rhythm that made polyphony impossible. There was but one rhythm possible at one and the same time since "filled-in" time and not an abstract unit of measurement formed its basis.

III

$\mathscr{J}$F POLYPHONY IN OUR SENSE of the word was unknown to the Greeks, did their music sound always as pure monophony? Or is it possible that they made use — if only occasionally — of "sound combinations," i. e., of different tones sounding together? This question cannot be answered with any degree of certainty since Greek music is no longer extant and cannot be recreated.

There are, to be sure, a few compositions which have come down to us in

Greek notation. However, they would scarcely suffice as a basis for the reproduction of Greek music as it sounded in antiquity — for various reasons. First, the number of compositions is much too small. From a consideration of these meager remnants we cannot hope to obtain a general picture of a music so completely different from our own. Second, all examples which have come down to us are of a later period; most of them belong to the post-Christian era, and even the oldest do not go back beyond the second century B.C. Even they, therefore, originated six centuries after Homer and two to three centuries after the great tragedians and Pindar. (The alleged melody of Pindar's first Pythian Ode is not authentic.) Third, we do not know — and this is the most important reason — what relationship existed between the notation and the actual sound in antiquity, for notation cannot be identified with music as sound; it is mute, it is not music.

In order to transform notation into music one must have a precise knowledge not only of the tone system, but also of all those unwritten conventions upon which the performance of the notated music was based. We know nothing of these conventions today, nor can such knowledge be acquired by purely theoretical procedures. One would have to know much more about the ancient practice of music and the rules applied in the transformation of notation into music. This is obviously not possible. We do not know today how the musician of ancient times produced music from notation, how he created sound, how (or whether) he varied the scheme of written notes, added to it or varied it — perhaps even by sound combinations. On the basis of the notation as it has come down to us, we cannot

surmise what musical meaning he extract-
ed from the notational scheme. It would
be false to reproduce music from the
ancient notation according to our modern
concept of music, and, for instance, to
identify ancient notes with modern tones
(say, with the tones of the piano) and to
execute them in the manner of today's
pieces written to be played from the
music, on the piano or on other instruments; to sing Greek music as we sing
ours today would be equally false. In
other words, the ancient notation must
not be converted to modern music.

Even though we have no idea as to how
the singing of our ode and the playing of
the aulos, which probably accompanied it,
actually sounded, we do find a certain
compensation in the contents of our poem,
for it contains an important reference to
the Greek conception of a certain type of
music. We have seen that the art of aulos

playing is described in our poem as the musical representation of mourning. The human cry of pain provided, according to this description, the impetus for the invention of aulos music. What is the aulos? It is a wind instrument on which one can play one part, and one part only. Such an instrument has a great resemblance to the human voice. Its tone, like that of the human voice, originates as a result of breath, of forced air. The voice, however, aside from being the transmitter of speech, also serves the utterance of affections. The outcry is audible life. Even if we do not speak, we can reveal our joy and our sorrow by means of the voice. The voice expresses the feelings of the subject, his joy and suffering, and it does so by means of the breath. The wind instrument has exactly the same capacity. Thus the aulos is capable of expressing something similar to that which is revealed by the voice; it can assume an attitude related to the expression of affections.

Over and above that, aulos playing is an art. The goddess Athena was so deeply impressed by the mourning of Euryales, the sister of Medusa (line 20), that she was impelled to preserve it, giving her impression a concrete and objective form. This overwhelming, heartrending impression of suffering as expressed through cries of mourning was represented by, or better, was represented as the aulos tune (*mimēsaito:* line 21). This impression was converted into art (*technē*), into ability, into aulos playing, into music. Athena wove this tune, as it were, out of the motives of mourning (*diaplexaisa:* line 8).

Pindar teaches us two things in this chorus: first, he distinguishes between suffering and the intellectual perception of suffering; the one, the actual expression of the affection, is human, is a characteristic of life, is life itself, whereas the other, the creation of an objective form by means of art, is divine, is liberating, is an intellectual deed. Only to the extent to which human beings possess this divine gift and are capable of receiving it from the hands of the goddess, as it were, are they granted access to the intellectual sphere. Second, Pindar tells us expressly that the music of the wind instrument is to be interpreted as the representation of human affections. This is important, for Pindar points to a definite origin of music and characterizes a particular type of music: music as the representation of expression. This music, then, is inherently just as monophonic as is the cry of the human and of the animal. We might say it is "linear."

Such music, like all other music, makes use of certain definite tones which bear a consonant relationship to each other (fourths and fifths). Aside from these tones which provide the skeleton of a melody, others are utilized which have the character of "in-between" tones. The latter cannot be expressed accurately through the diatonic system. They form intervals which can be expressed approximately as third- or quarter-tones. (The Greeks attempted to account for these tones through the so-called *chromatic* and *enharmonic* genera.) Their most essential characteristic, however, is precisely that they are not exactly measurable.

This irrational aspect of linear music is known to us from the exotic musical cultures of today. It reminds us strongly of the manner in which the voice breaks forth in an expression of affection. Hence it is highly characteristic of this type of music. Although the music of the aulos is characteristically monophonic, it is quite possible that monophony was not always strictly maintained, for, as a rule, the aulos is represented as a double aulos and it was possible to blow simultaneously into its two reeds. Probably one reed produced bourdon tones similar to those of the bagpipe.

The aulos was one of two typical musical instruments of the Greeks. The other was the lyre (kithara, phorminx), a stringed instrument, the sound of which originated from plucking or striking the strings. Sound combinations were possible in that several strings could be plucked simultaneously. One can readily understand that the art of playing such an instrument was not primarily a representation of subjective expression, of the outcry, of suffering. The magic exercised by such music can be compared more advantageously to sheer wonder at the sound per se. Exactly this wonder at the miracle of sound is here captured in art, the wonder that an object is capable of sounding, that an instrument can produce sounds — and sound combinations — i. e., sounds that fit, that suit one another. Therefore, the phenomenon of consonance is the very basis of lyre playing. Here, then, we do not deal primarily with linear music, but rather with music based on sound combinations *(klangliche Musik)*. In aulos playing the element of the subjective assumes shape, it represents our own activity, our own self, while the playing of the lyre makes us conscious of that which surrounds us. It captures the world as sound. Music here appears not as the representation of expression, but as the mirror of the harmony of the universe, which the awed human being discovers through the playing of an instrument. Since Pythagoras and his school and up to the time of Kepler, music was interpreted as the imperfect image, accessible to mankind, of that harmony of the spheres which was forever to remain inaccessible to human ears. Music was the image of inaudible sounds attributed to the planets.

A myth corresponding to the origin of aulos playing describes the origin of the lyre. The god Hermes is said to have invented it when he surmised that the shell of a turtle if used as a body of resonance could produce sound (Homeric Hymn to Hermes). The meaning of this myth is that the invention of the lyre is synonymous with the discovery of the universe as sound, with the discovery of the "sounding orbit." In this myth there are no traces whatsoever of a relationship between human-subjective expression and music.

These two basic concepts of music, described in the legends of Athena and

Hermes, both at the same time elementary and opposed to one another, contain all the possibilities of music. They are like two cornerstones on which all music rests to this day. They are the two extremes between which all music in history has oscillated. Characteristically, the lyre is the instrument of Homer, of the epos, of the serene contemplation of the universe, whereas the aulos is the instrument of exaltation and ecstasy, the instrument of the dithyramb. The lyre is the instrument of Apollo, the aulos, that of the Dionysiac festivals. In the classical period, as with Pindar, we find both instruments, the aulos and the lyre, and therefore both musical concepts, either separated or united.

In our chorus the tune invented by Athena and given to human beings is called a *nómos*, which later means "law." In music, however, this term had a special meaning: a basic concept of music underlying each individual realization. In other words, *nómos* means "model," the quintessence of the tune. Athena created the "divine" tune, the *polyképhalos nómos* (Many-heads-tune), and gave it to humans: this *nómos* is the prototype according to which the "human" tune originates each time anew through the art of the aulos player. The term *nómos,* accordingly, signifies not so much a definite tune as a definite species of tunes, one with a concrete musical content, to be sure, and within which different compositions may originate in practical execution.

The art of the musician, as is clear from the foregoing, does not lie in the invention of new pieces, of new tunes, but rather in the good, convincing and creative realization of the *nómos*. The *nómos* is like an ideal melody, actually nonexistent for it is divine, superhuman, but it invariably furnishes the basis for individual realization. It is comparable to an invisible theme from which variations are drawn. The activity of the musician, therefore, lies in providing variations on a given musical idea. This has nothing to do with free composition in the modern sense — as little as it has to do with the faithful performance of the ultimate details of a composition as such details are customarily expressed in modern notation. Musical activity in antiquity is comparable neither to our prevalent ideas of composition nor to those of performance. A certain analogy can perhaps be found in the practice of improvisation on the basis of certain fundamental ideas, or with a given musical skeleton as foundation. Greek notation corresponded probably to this basis only, to this skeleton, but not to the actual performance, not to the actual sound of this music. Therefore, Greek notation means so little to us.

There were, of course, a number of such *nómoi*, of such paradigms. Our *polyképhalos nómos*, with which Midas probably won the prize in the Pythian Games, is but one of the aulos *nómoi*. There were *nómoi* with song and others purely instrumental, yet the purely instrumental were exceptions for the Greeks since, as a rule, instruments were used for song and dance. The Greeks did not have a term at their disposal which would correspond to our word "music" and which they could have used — in the sense we do — to signify purely instrumental music. It is very illuminating, for example, that such a term is missing in our ode which treats of music — instrumental music. Pindar employs the terms *melos* (line 19) and *nómos* (line 23) for the instrumental aulos tune, and the aulos

50

player is not called a musician, but just an aulos player, an *auletes* (as stated in the heading of the ode).

IV

*M*USIC WAS CONNECTED MOST closely with the recitation of verse. Whenever Greek language sounded in verse, it was also a form of music. Does this mean that verse was always sung by the Greeks? Such a formulation of the question is not entirely correct, because Greek verse already *contains* music within itself; it need not be *set* to music. It was stated at the beginning that verse and music form a unified whole. Now let us see how it was possible that verse from its very origin was not only language but also music, without being expressly set to music, without being provided first with a special rhythm and a special melody. This strange admixture of verse and music, this unity, has its foundation in the Greek language itself. This is understandable because verse is not just language, but without any alteration also music, as a result of the fact that the language which forms the verse is not mere "language" in our sense, but possesses particular musical characteristics. This peculiar quality of Greek language is bound closely to Greek rhythm. (To what extent the melody of the Greek language may have contributed to this quality we are in no position to judge today, since we do not know Greek melody.)

We have seen that Greek rhythm knows no distinction between division of time and "filling-in" of rhythm. One uses the "ready-made" "physical bodies," the long and the short, the "filled-in" time, in order to compound rhythms. This rhythmic quality is not a characteristic feature of Greek music alone; it has not been freely invented, but is preformed in the peculiar quality of the Greek language. A passage from Plato's dialogue *Kratylos* makes that very clear: "Those who try their ability in rhythms distinguish first the functions of the letters, then of the syllables, and in this way they come to the rhythms in order to observe them, but not before." According to Plato, then, those who wish to concern themselves with rhythms must first have studied language, syntax, letters and syllables and must have an understanding of all of these. Why? Simply because the prototype of the rhythms is to be found in the language, in the syllables.

The Greek language is the prerequisite

of Greek rhythm. The syllables themselves are the rhythmic matter from which
a rhythm originates. Those small "physical bodies," those building stones, the
longs and the shorts, originate not by
means of abstract rhythmic division, but
from the language itself, and the individual syllables have definite duration in
the Greek language. They are either short
or long. This quality, inherent in the word
itself, is an essential feature of the *gestalt*
of the word. The fixed character of the
syllables is not carried into the word by
verse or musical rhythm, nor is it influenced by the individual speech, for it is an
objective feature of the word. It signifies
the word as a material carrier, as a body,
as an object. These long or short syllables
have nothing whatever to do with
individual desires for expression, nor do
they appear as a consequence of the
meaning of the word.

What we are trying to say can be better understood if one contrasts western languages with the Greek language. Take the word "father": the first syllable is accented and receives emphasis because emphasis expresses the meaning of the word, and "fa," the root syllable, carries that meaning. The second syllable, "ther," is light and is pronounced more quickly, since it is a mere ending and not so important for the meaning and for subjective expression. In English, then, as in any other western language neither the emphasis nor the length of the syllable conditioned by it, neither the lightness nor the brevity as exemplified in the word endings, are objective qualities of the word; they are not characteristics of the "word-body" itself, but instead are allied closely with the meaning, with the speaker and with what the speaker means to express. The accentuation and the lengthening of the syllable "fa" in "father," for instance, do not depend solely on the meaning of the word, but from case to case can be subjected to differing expression. One can say "father" or "faather" or "faaather," one can give the syllable more or less emphasis, differing weight.

This example clearly illustrates our point. In western languages the syllable itself is neither short nor long, but is *made* short or long by the speaker who forms it exactly as he wishes in order to invest it with meaning, with context, with emphasis, with affection. In this way, the close connection of the language to the subject is expressed, and for this reason, a syllable in a western language is neither short nor long per se. It is but relatively shorter, longer, very short or very long.

Only *one* feature of the word remains unalterable, the position of the accent:

"fáther." This position is fixed. In no situation imaginable would one say "fathér." The point (or place) in the word (or sentence) carrying the accent is comparable to a reinforced point, for the duration of this syllable is not fixed. That which is objective in western languages and independent of the will of the speaker, is alone this point. These languages delineate a sequence of accentuation, but the "filling-in" with definite duration differs throughout and is dependent upon the subject, upon the speaker.

The same word, "father," in Greek is "patēr." Each of these two syllables has its own, its fixed duration determined once and forever. This duration of the syllable is independent of the meaning and of the expression. It is equally independent of the will of the speaker, of the subject. It is objective. The word is rigid, it cannot be lengthened or contracted, it is like a solid body. This is a peculiar language indeed! In "pater" the main syllable, "pa," accented in English because it carries the meaning, in Greek is neither accented nor long, but the ending "ter," *is* long. In a different word it might be just the opposite because the regulation of the duration of a syllable is related neither to the significance of a syllable nor to the logical context; rather, it is related to the objective quality of the syllable itself. Characteristically enough, this quality is expressed even in the script, for Greek script distinguishes between short and long vowels. Thus an η is a long "e" (ē), and wherever it appears — irrespective of the meaning of the word, of the context and even of the expression — that syllable is long. Thus in the word mētēr (mother), for instance, both syllables are long.

Moreover, this quality has noteworthy

consequences: it may happen, for example, that mere endings or words relatively weak in meaning, such as articles and conjunctions, consist of long syllables. These syllables, as they are spoken, will of necessity occupy more time, will become more prominent than those syllables which to us appear much more important with respect to meaning. This circumstance becomes evident particularly when the main syllables are short. Let us look, for example, at the last two words of the first line of our ode. Each consists of three syllables. In each case the first two, the main syllables, are short, and only the two endings are long: brŏtĕān pŏlĭōn = mortal cities.

The endings of the words, as they are spoken here, take a dominant place, whereas the main parts go by almost unnoticed. According to our feeling for language, this is in contradiction to

meaning and expression. The speaker —
in our sense — would feel restricted. In
the second line, we found a noun which
consists only of two shorts: hĕdŏs (dwelling), and following it, a strictly transition-
al word which is long: hā (which). Thus
originates the strange — to our minds
even illogical — pronunciation: hĕdŏs hā
(dwĕllĭng which). This manner of speaking is illogical to us, because we are used
to associating length and accent with the
subject and we do not regard it merely as
a quality of the word-body. For the
Greeks, however, this manner of speaking
was correct. It was logical because the
speaker did not feel the "long" as emphasis; the "long" was an incidental quality
of the *gestalt* of the word.

We must understand that the verse
"behaves" like language because the
verse *is* language. It can employ and give
shape only to what is already contained in

language. Greek verse is formed from
Greek words, from Greek sentences.
That which distinguishes it from daily
language is that words are chosen in
such a manner as to realize a definite,
pre-existent sequence of longs and
shorts. (It is possible, of course, that
in ordinary speech these long and short
syllables were not in a rational, arithmetic relationship to each other, and that
only in verse the relationship of the long
to the short syllable became gradually
stylized. One can compare the syllables
in ordinary speech to stones which, though
unpolished, nonetheless have fixed dimension. In verse, the syllables may be
compared to polished stones, to small
cubes, as it were, in the relationship of
$2 : 1$, or also of $1\frac{1}{2} : 1$.) In the last line of
our strophe, for example, the words and
syllables have been so chosen that by
means of their inherent long and short

syllables, the given sequence of longs and shorts is rendered tangible. The last line of the last strophe has a momentous, an elevated meaning: unexpectedly time will grant one favor but yet not another. Nevertheless, this high-minded meaning is the very element which cannot be expressed either by the speaker or by the form of the verse, and here it appears as something independent of the desire of the speaker, something as unalterable as Fate herself. The meaning, in the last analysis, thereby appears incomprehensible to humans, just as does the origin of Greek words, of the Greek word-body. The meaning of this line is just as inflexible as are the Greek words, which can be influenced neither by the subject nor by his desire for expression. They have their own will. They are incapable of receiving, carrying or expressing emphasis. Consequently, the line as a whole allows no coloring, no variation, no interpretation, no supplementation through sound. It is a fixed *gestalt*, as are the Greek words themselves.

When saying that the verse cannot stand alteration, interpretation or supplementation by sound, we mean that an independent rhythm cannot be joined to it according to the rhythmic principles of music, for an independent rhythmic musical composition would necessitate some manner of alteration of the verse, of that fixed *gestalt*, and that is not possible. The statement that the verse allows no supplementation through musical rhythm means simply that the verse already contains musical rhythm. And so it is: one cannot supplement Greek verse by applying musical rhythm to it because verse does not require supplementation and, on the other hand, the word rhythm is musically established through the language,

and entirely so: thus the rhythm of the
above-quoted last line, for instance, is
♩ ♩ ♩ ♩ ′ ♩ ♩ ♩ ♩ ′ ♩ ♩ ♩ ♩.
Greek verse by its very nature is not only
a linguistic, but at the same time a
musico- rhythmic reality. Still better, the
rhythm in linguistic respect — linguistic,
to be sure, in the Greek sense of the word
— is completely established also as regards "music." Therefore nothing further
would be accomplished by adding a
special, a musical rhythm. Greek verse
contains musical components because of
the very nature of the Greek language.

This can be understood better when
one realizes the character of western
verse. Like Greek verse, that of western
civilization is founded on the quality of
the language which forms its basis. We
have noted that in western languages only
the position of the accent is fixed "objectively," and we have compared this

position to a "point." The rhythmic "filling-in" of detail, i.e., the actual rhythmic proportions, in each case depends upon the speaker. The same holds true of western verse, it is distinguished from daily language only in that it prescribes a definite number of syllables together with a more or less fixed order of accentuation.

O, mistress mine, where áre you róaming? (Shakespeare, Twelfth Night)

Western languages, and therefore western verse, have a certain resemblance to the principle of the musical measure: they fix a sequence of accentuation comparable to a sequence of accented (•) and unaccented (·) points. Beyond that the verse shows another resemblance to the musical measure: it determines an *order* of accentuation, that is, a regular repetition of fixed sequences of accents, for example,

· • · • · • , etc., • · · • · · • · · , etc.

(One even has the feeling that the accents take place at identical time-intervals — as in the measure — although objectively this is not the case.) In western languages and western verse, as in western music, the establishment of the rhythm does not take place at *one* time and conclusively, as in the Greek language, but occurs, as it were, in two different layers, in two successive "work-shifts": first, the order of accentuation is determined, then the "filling-in" with a concrete rhythm takes place. In language, this "filling-in" is not objectively determinable; in music, it employs rhythmic values objectively measurable.

The common character of western languages and western music has still another important consequence: the strict differentiation between the rhythm of the language and that of the music, which made the autonomy of musical rhythm possible. In language and verse only the succession of accents is objectively determined, while the rhythmic "filling-in" is a correlate of the word meaning, the logical context and the expression, etc.; it is associated with the speaker. In other words, it depends in each case upon the speech, and is a strictly *linguistic* phenomenon. It is not fixed musically. Musical rhythm has other means at its disposal. It is therefore possible to determine the subjective rhythmic values of the language in an objective musical sense (as long as one preserves the order of accentuation). Thus it is possible to set a verse to music with a specific rhythm, and that is necessary indeed if the verse is to be set to music at all. In the setting the autonomy of the musical rhythm is shown most clearly by the fact that one has different possibilities at his disposal. For instance,

O, mistress mine, where are you roaming?

Western language and western music, and thereby the intellectual attitude which lies at their base, are such that the rhythm of language and that of music are not identical and cannot be identical, but are two different and autonomous things. The verse, therefore, allows independent rhythmic musical composition, and indeed demands it. Precisely this is impossible in Greek verse, and for the same reason Greek verse is both language and music.

Still another result is produced by the fact that the Greek *gestalt* of the word determines the rhythm independently of content: sentence and thought do not terminate necessarily with the strophe.

The effect is not that of an artistic device, such as the enjambment — the running over of a sentence from one line into the next — and it is not at all artificial. It should be regarded, instead, as the natural consequence of the Greek structure of language and verse. In our ode it occurs in all transitions to the next strophe. A parallel in the realm of western music would be possible only in a manner of composing in which the music would not intend to do justice to the thought and context of the language. Something of this order is found in the isorhythmic motet of the 14th century in France, in the works of Guillaume de Machaut. There one frequently finds an exact repetition of the rhythmic scheme in all parts without such scheme becoming evident in the melodic line through caesura or repetition.

V

*T*HUS FAR WE HAVE
concerned ourselves with rhythm in both
music and language. We have seen that
the Greeks knew a peculiar kind of
rhythm, which does not distinguish
between accent and duration, and a
peculiar language, which does not distinguish between music and language. We,
however, do not possess this rhythm or
language and are not acquainted with it
through immediate experience. It is not
enough to describe this rhythm theoreti-

cally, because rhythm — and therefore music — cannot be understood or "possessed" through mere description. Rhythm — and music — is never present as a finished product, but exists only momentarily, as action. Only when one can assume a rhythmic attitude similar to that of the Greeks, when one can render a language such as Greek in conformity with its peculiar demands, only then can one understand these patterns — through one's own action, with the theoretical knowledge being but auxiliary.

If we want to draw the consequences from these statements, we find ourselves in a difficult situation from which there seems no escape. We do not know how the Greek language sounded, nor do we know what sort of melody was connected with it. We know but one thing: ancient Greek is spoken incorrectly today, and can only be spoken thus by modern Greeks as well as by Englishmen, Americans, Germans and Frenchmen. They do not pronounce it as Greek, but rather according to the rules and habits of their own languages. We have seen, however, that all western languages by their very nature are irreconcilable with Greek. They are "pure" languages, whereas Greek has its own musico-rhythmic quality. When we recite Greek verse today as "language" we can do so only in the western sense: we can think of the "accent" as objective — and since the accent is not fixed in Greek verse, we execute the long with an accent. The actual rhythmic "filling-in" becomes dependent on the subjective aspects of the recitation, becomes a correlate of meaning and of expression. It is therefore executed incorrectly, in a manner contradictory to the character of Greek language. Exactly in this manner is the rhythm of Greek verse performed today. The longs and shorts are executed freely, as if they were merely a result of the recitation. No rational relationship, such as 2 : 1, no musical rhythm is applied.

What can we do under such circumstances? Is it at all possible to render Greek verse correctly, according to its own peculiar character? There is no hope of reproducing this verse, hence the original character of the Greek language, of realizing it exactly as did the ancient Greeks; nor is there any point in attempting it, because, as we have said, rhythm, music, and also language as sound are not finished products but exist rather as action, as activity. They exist only in our presence, as utterances of our own individual selves. During the time of their realization they are identical with the self, with the individual. It is therefore pointless to try to reconstruct Greek verse with "historical correctness," or to at-

tempt to render it with exactness. We
lack the basic premise: man today simply
is not identical with the ancient Greeks.
However, we can strive for one thing: to
realize the phenomena of the past as correctly as possible on the basis of an insight
into their essential characteristics; this
means to make them present, vital and
valid for us today. One can do no more,
but one should do no less. This attitude
demands scholarly methods and historical
knowledge, imagination, artistic ability
and, above all, responsibility toward
historical data — things not to be taken
for granted.

Let us apply this demand to Greek
verse: we must render it in such a way
that everything we have established
above becomes valid. First, the nature of
the rhythm is musical, and the rhythm, as
such, exactly determined; it must be
interpreted and performed with musical

exactitude. Second, this rhythm lies in the objective *gestalt* of the word; it has nothing to do with the manner in which western languages are spoken, this manner being conditioned by meaning. The consequence of the first statement is strict rhythmic scansion, which, applied to the first line, for instance, is:

♩ ♩ ♩ ♩ ♩ ♩ ♩ ♩ ♩ ♩ ♩ ♩ ♩ ♩

Is this logical if one continues to "speak," that is, if one continues to employ only that melody which is natural to the languages of today, a rise and fall in tone which is independent of music, of actual melody? Is this type of "speaking chorus" logical in connection with a musical rhythm? Definitely not, for a musical rhythm demands musical pitches. Aside from that, such rendition, despite the musical rhythm, would give the effect of speaking in the modern sense and would violate the second of the two points made above. An inflection resulting only from speech is bound to condition the performance through meaning and expression; it is inseparably connected with the process of speaking in the modern western sense. One cannot associate the idea with it that rhythm is inherent in the objective *gestalt* of the word. The more we try to render Greek "correctly" within this framework, the further we remove ourselves from the true nature of the Greek language. Besides, we stand in continual danger of abandoning the strict musical rhythm and falling back into a speaking rhythm which would be a correlate of meaning and expression. This happens whenever one attempts to "recite" Greek verse in modern times.

Only one thing can help us: we eliminate speaking as we know it; that is, we introduce not only musical rhythm, but also musical tonal sequence, and we shall reveal Greek verse as what it was: language and music at the same time. Even though we do not know the melody, not even the general type of Greek melody, we must introduce one (albeit for negative reasons, namely, in order to eliminate mistakes resulting from speech inflection). We should not be led astray by the ambition to reconstruct an ancient melody; on the contrary, we know that that is impossible. We shall therefore introduce a melody as neutral as possible, one so inconspicuous that it will not be disturbing: let us simply introduce a succession of tones which corresponds more or less to the rhythmic *gestalt* of the verse. It should serve only to aid us in our conception of Greek verse as a reality to which we commit ourselves — as far as possible and so that all that we have considered historically logical is real-

izable. This succession of tones should be
nothing more than an aid; it should
merely sustain the verse. Since we are
aware that this succession is historically
incorrect, its employment is not as bad as
it would be to recite verse incorrectly in
ignorance, or at least without awareness
of false recitation. We employ these
pitches only in order to exclude other,
more grave mistakes. Turning to our ode:
we have included a succession of tones in
the Appendix for one strophe. In doing so
we have paid no heed to the vague clues
given us by Greek musical theory. We
should prefer to avoid any resemblance
to ancient Greek music, for it could be
only misleading and superficial. The
succession more nearly resembles the
church modes as employed in the monophonic music of the Christian church.
Nevertheless, such a succession permits
us the rendition of the verse as song so

that it is freed from the bonds of meaning and expression conditioning recitation. We must advance far enough in this direction to enable us to feel Greek words themselves as objective even in their material, verbal *gestalt,* to feel them as filled with fixed musical rhythm, as "fixed quantities." We must experience Greek syllables, words and sentences not only as musical rhythm, but as "filled-in" time, in short, as *Greek* rhythm. We must comprehend the static character of Greek rhythm not only from the purely musical aspect, but, above all, as the essential feature of the rhythm of Greek language; we must relive the origin of rhythm step by step, by the juxtaposition of long and short syllables with no dynamic inflection whatsoever and without movement which would condition expression. Such re-experiencing would also regulate the tempo, and in such a way that the small temporal unit, the short, would remain concrete, something autonomous (i. e., not faster than, let us say, $\cup$ = 90 M. M.). In this way we might at last perceive and represent Greek verse as a fixed *gestalt* including all the features of a solid body of definable dimension.

VI

*I*F THE FOREGOING CAN BE achieved, one will understand the unity which verse forms not only with music but with the dance as well. To experience words and verse as solid bodies, as something physical, means automatically to experience them *through* the body, physically. Since verse expresses itself in time, as the molding of time, as movement, its physical character expresses itself as visible physical movement, as dance.

This holds true also for the odes of Pindar. They were not only recited but at the same time were realized through the movement of the chorus. Pindar's lines were not only music, but also dance; they were not only poetry, not only song but *choréia,* that is, "the total of dance and song." This is the definition given by Plato *(Laws).* A passage from Aristotle *(Metaphysics),* too, clearly demonstrates that for the Greeks rhythm was intimately connected with the feeling for the physical as a quality and that it could not be thought of as an abstract, purely musical phenomenon: he gives examples of the smallest units of measurement and employs the step and the syllable for rhythms. It does not occur to him to mention the "short," that is, a purely musical element, as probably we would specify a note value, the quarter or the eighth and so on, or as we would designate

83

even an absolute, abstract value of time according to the metronome.

The contents of our chorus — of our *choréia* — also allude twice to the *chorós* (lines 26 and 27.) It would be incorrect to translate this word as "dance" or "round," for in antiquity, in the works of Homer, Pindar, or in the Greek tragedy, *chorós* meant round dance with song. The meaning of this word, however, is divided in our time: in modern Greek it means "dance," in the other western languages "choral song" (e. g., choir, *choeur, coro, Chor*).

It may well prove interesting to follow the changes of meaning which this word *chorós* has undergone in the course of centuries, for thereby light is cast upon the changes in intellectual attitude and manner of thinking from antiquity to western civilization. In early Christianity the old Greek meaning of the word was applied to the celestial spheres, and one spoke of "angelic choirs." A derivative of it was the choir of the priests: the corresponding part of the church is termed "choir" to this day. It is important, however, that associations of both singing and motion helped shape all these terms. One always had the feeling of something happening in space. The singing choir separated itself from the clerical choir. As a result, the meaning of the word became more narrow inasmuch as the conception of movement in space no longer applied. In later times, the singing choir even left the choir of the church and occupied the loft, the opposite side, which established its lay character even more firmly. Finally, we should mention the customary use — today — of the word "chorus" in such terms as "opera chorus" or "church chorus."

Let us refer to the passage in our ode

which makes reference to the *chorós* (henceforth we shall use the word "chorus" in the ancient sense of *choréia*). Pindar describes how the aulos tune, the *polyképhalos nómos,* was originated by the goddess Athena as the reflection of the sorrowful cries of the sisters of Medusa. He imagines this tune streaming through the aulos and assuming concrete form as a result of human action. How concrete, how corporeal is this representation! Indeed a solid union of human feeling and divine creativity! Here is a unified idea, complete in itself, of human-divine action, i. e., of intellectual reality! It is a profound interpretation of music as *present* action, solely through the use of the present tense of the verb: flowing through *(dianisómenon;* line 25). Pindar "sees" the aulos before him, it is physically present in his imagination, and he wants to make it tangible also to us: as something existent and as something that has originated — molded copper and reeds. The aulos does not lie before us as a lifeless object, but rather it is fused with human activity: the tune streams through the copper and the reed. Nor do these reeds grow just anywhere; they grow in the holy district near the city of Charites, the city with the beautiful round dances, near Lake Kephisís (Kopais) in Boethia (line 26 f): "consecrated" reeds, therefore, which are ready to vibrate with the moving air as the tune streams through them. These reeds are the "faithful witnesses" of the *choreutes* (line 27), "faithful witnesses" in a twofold sense: due to the place where they grow (near the city with the beautiful round dances), and due to the function they exercise as components of the aulos, participating in the round dances, and accompanying them. The *choreutes* sustain the round dance, embody it and manifest it: singers and dancers at the same time. They dance on that soil from which the reeds grow; they form the connection with the consecrated earth. Pindar in this ode presents us with a unity, self-evident to him and therefore realistic-plastic, a unity of human suffering, instrumental play, poetry, singing and dancing. The divine origin legitimates not only the human action, but even an otherwise lifeless object, the aulos with the reed mouthpiece.

Can we possibly imagine this choral movement? That Greek rhythm was physically experienced is shown by such terms as *foot, thesis* and *arsis. Pous* (foot) is step and also a unit of measurement. With reference to rhythm, foot is a definite combination of longs and shorts, easily recognized by the regularity of repetition. The dactyl (— ∪∪), for example, is a foot, as is the iambus (∪ —). *Thesis* (descent) refers to putting the foot on the ground, *arsis* (ascent) to lifting it. Thus the dactyl could be divided into *thesis* and *arsis:* long (thesis) and two shorts (arsis). In the more complex rhythms which, as in our ode, do not originate through regular repetition of one foot, we do not know exactly how the ancient Greeks divided thesis and arsis. For this reason alone — even if we knew everything else — we cannot reconstruct the ancient movement, any more than we can reconstruct the ancient melody. Nor should we strive here (any more than in the case of melody) for a reconstruction faithful to the original. We must realize this choral singing as movement, as motion valid for us, in order to experience it as physically as possible — as did the ancients. We do not want to reconstruct the "correct" steps. We strive to comprehend only the reality of choral singing — and it is none

other than the verse, the language itself —
as a living, total thing. We must make
this attempt, even at the expense of
"correct" steps, just as we did in the
introduction of tonal intervals. Such a
procedure is preferable to no movement
at all, and can even be very profitable
provided we do not succumb to the
temptation of introducing a movement
contradicting our historical knowledge.
Such a procedure is commensurate with
historical conscience.

As a suggestion for the performance of
our ode, for example, we can execute the
two shorts or the single short each time as
an arsis: on each of the first two longs we
complete a step, first with the left foot,
then with the right; on each of the first
two shorts, we touch the ground lightly
with the left toe, without transferring our
weight to this foot, and only on the succeeding long do we complete a step with

the left foot and proceed further: ⌞ _r_ ⁽ˡ⁾
⁽ˡ⁾ ⌞ . Passages such as this: _r_ ⁽ˡ⁾ ⌞ _r_ .
would be executed correspondingly. On
the short we would touch the floor once
with the toe before completing the step
with the same foot on the succeeding long.
This basic scheme can take on concrete
form through movements forward and
backward, to the right and to the left, etc.,
movements which correspond to the form
of the line and the strophe.

The physical-objective quality of the
Greek word, its existence independent of
the subjective will, can produce its effect
only through physical realization, and
that effect is an emanation of its existence
which remains mysterious, and of its origin which remains hidden from us. The
word which is not just spoken or not just
sung, but which is actually, physically
realized, assumes an almost magical
presence, and in none of the modern west-

ern languages do we find anything even remotely comparable.

VII

*W*HAT IS THE SECRET REASON for the existence and effect peculiar to Greek language and verse? We have stated frequently that it lies in the musical component of the Greek language, in the unity formed by language and music. Before attempting to describe the significance of this unity and how it was perceived by the ancients, we must become aware of what language and speech mean today and of the manner in which we employ language as the bearer of meaning.

Through language we designate things
and render them somehow tangible. We
determine the significant contexts. In this
process our means are phonetic, and we
use words consisting of vowels and
consonants. These means are purely linguistic, that is, they can serve speech
exclusively, they are entirely coordinated
with our linguistic capacity. The vowels
do not have the quality of musical tone
for they are associated neither with definite pitches nor with definite pitch
successions, indeed, they dare not be, for
they would thereby lose their purely
phonetic character. Neither do they have
an autonomous rhythmic quality. The
consonants are similarly formed. They
are sounds serving the unequivocal for-
mations of the words. They are means of
articulation. They are chiefly the means
which can achieve concreteness through
language, to such an extent that that

94

which we term language originates: the designation of things, of perceptions, of meaning — a store of unequivocal symbols for the human capacity of designation. The sounding aspect of the language, the mere sound of the word, therefore, the phonetic element, the process of speaking, are intimately bound up with the meaning of the word on the one hand, and with the subject and the subjective expression on the other. The sound of the word has no autonomous function of its own directed toward the world of the senses, for language as mere sound becomes almost devoid of significance if we do not connect it with meaning, if we do not, indeed, understand the language as language, if we listen, for example, to a language with which we are unfamiliar. Speech makes sense to us only insofar as we are able to associate the sound with an experience of meaning. Neither is an autonomous force inherent in the mere sound of poetry, such as it is, for example, in the substance of music or of painting. For — to remain in the realm of music — the substance of music, a consonance or a musical rhythm, such as the rhythm of a Bach subject, possesses a rational structure and therefore allows itself to be communicated. The musical intervals and rhythms address the world of the senses directly, and it is not necessary to relate them to a particular content in order to comprehend them as meaningful. The situation is similar in the other arts, for instance, in reference to colors and lines. Therefore, whereas in poetry the tie to the object is established through a linguistic experience of meaning, objectivation takes place in the other arts through a lawfulness inherent in the sensual material — the tones, the rhythms, the colors, the lines, etc.

The Greek language, too, contains all the above-mentioned features of a language. Like our own speech, that of the Greeks was, of course, a phonetic phenomenon. But it was more: it retained a musical "sound-body," one conditioned not only linguistically, in the narrow sense of the word, but one which, like music and the other arts, functioned autonomously due to its immediate ties to the world of the senses.

Let us recall our previous observations: musical sound-bodies and language to the Greeks were a unity. We experience this entity in the form of Greek rhythm. The roots of this rhythm extend as far back as to the dance *(órchesis),* to the feeling of the corporeal, to the realm of the preintellectual and the purely instinctive. It addresses human beings from the most elementary level of the purely physical-motile to the highest level of logic, of the language.

In antiquity the rhythmic-musical capacity directly related to the world of the senses was realized not only in music and in dance, but, above all, in the intellectually most advanced means of utterance, the word itself. Accordingly, we do not deal with a language which enters into an alliance with music and with dance, as is possible in modern languages. Nor do we deal with a poetry which forms the basis of a composition and which can also be danced or given choreographic representation. The activity of the Greek creator of verse, of choruses, cannot be compared with that of a modern poet-composer such as Richard Wagner, for the making of verse already contains a musical aspect, at least with respect to rhythm (we know nothing about the other, melody), and it is, at the same time, a "composing" of the verse in the musical sense. The "filled-in" time of the syllables renders the word fixed as a body in that it has an existence within the word which is not concerned with the language proper. Although that time is not a linguistic quality in the narrower sense of the word, it cannot be separated from the Greek word. We cannot isolate it.

The distinguishing characteristic of ancient Greek lies in the realization of the word as an independent rhythmic-musical force and at the same time as language, as a phonetic structure, as a vehicle of perceptions and affections. The word appears not only phonetically appropriate, but it is something more: a rational artistic substance formed for its own sake; it is sound, song. It is "language," to be sure, like our own, inasmuch as it serves the delineation of meaning and context, but, through a quality which is scarcely intelligible to us any more, it is, like music, directly related to the senses. It is a rhythm which, independent of its linguistically conditioned character as mere sound, lends solidity to the word, a solidity that comes from another sphere. Similar qualities must have been inherent in ancient Greek also with reference to the tone.

The autonomous element of music forms a unity with the element of language conditioned by meaning. It forms a reality of its own uniting linguistic precision of meaning with autonomous musical force. Thus ancient Greek was doubly anchored: in the concreteness of meaning, absent from autonomous artistic matter, such as music, and which would enable it to represent substance and to reveal the essence of actual things, as it were; and in the autonomous power of the artistic substance with its immediate effect upon the senses, absent from lan-

guage and which likewise would enable it
to represent the essence of things. Ancient
Greek was a peculiar vehicle of meaning.
It was like a music which at the same time
had the capacity of designating things.

How did the Greeks feel about their
own language? They must have had the
feeling that they were not entirely its
masters, for Greek could not be made
entirely to coincide with the human's
narrower capacity for speech. Something
always remained: the "filled-in" time of
syllables and words. This something, this
substratum of the Greek syllables, words
and sentences, cannot be obliterated, cannot be absorbed into our own capacity for
language; it is always present, regardless
of our will. It emerges again and again,
no matter how thoroughly we erase our
linguistic blackboard. This substratum,
this fixed *gestalt* of the word, imposes

itself upon us like a spirit which appears independent of our will. It has its own rhythmic will not obeying the linguistic will of the speaker. Therefore the word leads, in addition, a life independent of human linguistic capacity, it evidences its own substance, and with that substance the Greeks were confronted. In other words, they must have had the feeling that the objects are not named by humans, but that they manifest themselves, their own substance, in sound.

As a result, some elemental consciousness of magic lives in the Greek language, and in the Greek intellect as well. We find a situation in which the things of the outer and inner world meet us as active and living forces, as "essence." Objects here behave like animate beings and feelings are objectified, personified. There is no distinction between conception and name,

on the one hand, and object and individual
material thing, on the other. The field is
open to conjuration.

The ancient Greek word, as a consequence, is much closer to the realm
of magic than are the western languages.
Nevertheless, it does not remain im-
prisoned in it; it no longer belongs to
a "magical culture," for the conscious
comprehension and creation of the word
as the highest intellectual vehicle of
meaning, such as the activity of Homer
himself, has overcome that phase. The
possibility of a logic already exists in the
Greek word. In Greek logic, however, in
the philosophy of Plato, intellectual
concept and the object perceptible to the
senses are intimately associated one with
the other. The idea is presented as
substance perceived by means of our
senses. One cannot abstract it from the
object. The idea is "hypostatized," that

is, it obtains a quasi-material *gestalt,* as it were. Thus Greek logic aims at a direct comprehension of the "essence of things." It is a "logic of being," that is, an "ontology." It can be ontological due to the character of Greek language — because one perceives objects through the language as if they themselves manifested their substance (as we have seen). In western languages, however, the ontological aspect of the word has vanished, as it were. Western philosophy has evolved correspondingly: logic has separated itself from ontology; the "essence of things," understood by the Greeks as substance and as present, in Kant's philosophy was transformed to the *Ding an sich,* the thing per se, which remains inaccessible to the human.

The Greek language therefore brings with it. that peculiar intellectual capacity according to which one has the feeling that he perceives the essence of the thing itself. The substance is concentrated in corporeity. It becomes palpable to the senses. And vice versa: the object of the senses is not a mere representation of a substance itself inaccessible, but rather is "being" itself. For the Greeks the realm of the intellectual, of the substantial, is lowered to that of the sensory and becomes identical with it. The ancient conception of "being" is characterized, as Hegel says, by the consciousness of the "god himself entering the temple and dwelling in our midst." *(Der Gott wohnt seiner Äußerlichkeit ein — Aesthetik,* Einleitung). It is the age of the plastic arts. "In truth they (the gods) come themselves, and men become accustomed to good fortune and to daylight and to gaze upon the manifest," says Hoelderlin *(Brot und Wein).* We deal here with much more than artistic creations in the western sense, namely, with the almost corporeal presence of intellectuality, a situation through which the god himself becomes, as it were, accessible to the senses. Thus the plastic arts for the Greeks are more than mere arts, and one has the impression that the statues themselves are beings and that they possess substitutive power.

The ancient Greek word, too, comes to us, one might say, as a plastic reality. It exists as a solid body and, so to speak, is tangible. The words of a Greek verse hit us as though they were stones. This is the effect, too, of the words of prayers which, by their mere existence, i. e., by their sound, effect fulfillment. In this manner we must understand the beginning of our chorus: when Pindar entreats the city of Agrigent, invoked at the same time as an active being, to receive the victor with the laurel wreath, one has the impression that the words could actually bring about what they express. They can cause the prayer to be heard; they have, as it were, the power of conjuration.

This powerful instrument of meaning was at the disposal of the Greek poets. Is the designation "poet" correct? Can one call the Greek art of verse-making "poetry" in the sense in which we designate a work of Shakespeare or of Dante? Obviously not, but today we have no other term for it. The ancients, however, possessed the adequate term: *musikē*. It expresses the peculiar character of those works and at the same time designates the intellectual capacity of the Greeks allied with it. It can be translated neither as "music" nor as "poetry." The word *musikē* in Greek is an adjective, not a noun. It means *mus-ish,* "pertaining to the Muses." Perhaps one could amplify it: "mus-ish activity" or "mus-ish education." Possibly it would be best to connect the two: "mus-ish education through mus-ish activity," for *musikē* implies a deed, an activity, and not a finished product. This activity, as we have seen before, characterizes music in general. Whereas we classify music with the arts, *musikē* was not understood by the Greeks as an "art" in our sense of the word. Since its roots extend directly into the realm of the sensual and instinctive, and since it is *logos* at the same time, it cannot be absorbed entirely by the category of aesthetics, but lays claim also to that of ethics. Thus Plato understood *musikē* as an educational force, and antiquity, in general, looked upon *musikē* in this sense. This was possible only because *musikē* was founded on that peculiar agent of meaning, the Greek language. Pindar calls aulos playing *technē,* "art" (line 8), but he does not term art the chorus, *musikē,* which is conveyed by language.

The seeming contradiction may be explained thus: though in antiquity music as an individual art did not obtain anywhere near the place it has occupied in western civilization, *musikē* functioned, nevertheless, as the very essence of intellectual education and as the force determining the ethos. Only if we overlook the power of the Greek *musikē* to determine the human in his totality, only if we regard it as just poetry or music in the modern sense — which would be erroneous — only then could we designate it as art in our sense of the word.

Musikē was an educative force for still another reason. We have seen that the ancient Greeks had no influence over the words through enunciation, that they could not modify them, bend them to their purposes, or make them serve their expression. They could not even emphasize meaning. The words stand rigid, sphinxlike, put together like the stones of a mosaic. They form rigid figures and are in no manner whatever attachable to subjects. Much less can they be blended into a unity with the subject. Greek language is like a language of masks, it has no similarity to living facial expression. Such languages still exist in exotic cultures. One cannot penetrate the meaning of the speaker, one does not know whether he has good or bad intentions, whether he is gay or angry. Similarly sphinxlike, masklike — to us — are the faces in such cultures as the Siamese, for instance. The Greek language has the same effect as the mask in the Greek tragedy. Here, too, the power of its substance is by no means weakened by the absence of a spontaneous human facial expression; on the contrary, it achieves full validity only through such absence. Identical was the effect of the Greek word, which could have a powerful, bestial, demoniac, evocative sound, but never a subjective one in the western sense, never an intimate sound, shaded with fine nuances, or a bombastic sound. The pathos conditioned by content which often gains admittance in the act of recitation is foreign to the Greek word.

Only when one grasps the full import of the static character of the Greek word can one do justice to its essential, specifically Greek content. Only then does one understand, for instance, why the Greek sentence is determined much more by the static noun than by the dynamic verb. In particular, the Greek word order within the sentence, which seems so peculiar to us, becomes intelligible. It is impossible, for example, to "speak" a sentence like this: Φερσεφονας εδος, α τ' οχθαις επι μηλοβοτου ναιεις 'Ακραγαντος ευδματον κολωναν, ω ανα,

This fact becomes clearer when we retain the Greek word order in the translation: "Persephone's home that and [the] hilltops on [of the] sheep-pasturing dost inhabit Akragas' fair-built crest, oh Queen."

It is the quality of the static musical rhythm, of the "filled-in" time which makes this unbelievably free word order possible. It is wrong to see in such sentences a highly intricate dynamic system of relationships and to try to "speak" them accordingly — as so frequently is done. The coherence of the sentence is not vouchsafed through a dynamic placement of the words within it, as is the case in English, for instance, but is present only latently (determined, to be sure, also by the manifold endings of a highly differentiated system of inflection). We must allow the individual words to affect us in their static nature; only then will the unity of the context arise through our own intellectual activity, an activity which in western languages we are spared. The Greek language demands a different mental capability: the words, freely strewn about, in a sense, must be held together by the element of static rhythm, devoid of meaning. Precisely this feature must have been present in a language of that kind to an extent which is and must remain unknown to us today. Words were juxtaposed, and meaning was allowed to originate without the slightest support from speech. Since the words, these rigid bodies, could not be blended into a unity of meaning by the speaker, this was left to mental activity, or better: the word order challenged the mental activity, this collaboration between the "objectively" placed words and the individual.

For this reason, too, *musikē* had an

immense educative power. The individual was forced to participate actively not only as a speaker, but as a listener as well. Both parts had to engage in the same mental activity, a factor of far-reaching significance: Greek language and Greek verse presuppose, and have the power to form a communion, and that power is no longer understandable to us today. The separation of active speakers from passive listeners, easily possible today, is unthinkable in the Greek communion. A sorcerer leading and playing upon a dull crowd of people, a dichotomy of modern times, is impossible in the society which was the carrier of Greek verse. With utmost intellectual alertness everyone participated actively in the performance of that physically organized, rigid conveyor of meaning which we call Greek verse. Imagine all that such a conveyor of meaning, the *musikē,* was capable of stating, provoking, presenting and realizing, things nonexistent in the modern capacity of representation, in the modern conveyors of meaning.

VIII

$\mathcal{A}$NCIENT GREEK WAS A language spoken by humans, however, and, transformed into modern Greek, lives on today. How, then, did it happen that it lost these characteristics, that it has changed so completely? Why does nothing similar exist in any of the modern languages? How could it be that the ancient Greek attitude toward language and with it the ancient Greek intellectuality, have vanished?

The beginnings of such change probably date from a fairly early period: toward the end of the fifth century, B.C., that is, during the blossoming period of the classical antiquity, one finds certain signs which can furnish clues. In that time, the "new dithyramb" came into being, and its innovations excited conservative minds. Phrynis and Timotheos were reproached for allowing the music of this new dithyramb to become too independent, to go its own way. Here probably began a distinction between "writing" poetry and "composing" music, most evident in the rhythm: heretofore language alone had determined the rhythm. The relation of the long to the short syllables had followed the model of language; now the syllables were treated more freely and the innovators employed, in addition to the normal long (— = ♩ or ♩.) other values, "hyper-longs," which could have

117

a duration three or four times as long as that of the short ($\cup$ = $\quad$), therefore $-$ = $\quad$ or $\quad$ The aging Euripides was among these innovators. The comedian Aristophanes, a conservative, chided him by presenting, for instance, a passage from Euripides' *The Frogs* with stuttering: "ei-ei-ei-eilissousa cheroin." This syllable "ei" is obviously a "hyper-long" in Euripides' work, and from that Aristophanes derived his witticism. To him and his audience the long-holding of the syllable was incomprehensible; he could fill in this long duration only through repetition of the syllable giving the effect of stuttering.

Plato also advocated the unity of *musikē*. He fought the new movement, one for which he had little respect. He believed in the solidity of the Greek word-body and in an intellectual attitude belonging thereto. Only in that manner can we understand his concept of *musikē* as a force forming the ethos of humans.

This change in the treatment of verse and music possibly went hand in hand with the change of language itself, and indeed would have been impossible had the language not helped it along by creating the basis for such changes. In turn, the change in the language points to a change in intellectuality. The edifice of Greek education, of the Greek intellect, of Greek reality, of Greek existence began to totter. Slowly the foundations of a new and different epoch were formed. The language lost its fixed rhythm and therefore its character as a solid body. The words lost their willfulness. They no longer offered strong resistance. They became shadowy and could be fitted not only to a musical rhythm of its own, but also to the wishes of the speaker. They became willing and flexible tools in his service. The way was paved for a new manner of speaking, for that which we today understand as "speaking," a speaking tone which serves the expression of meaning and context and which, beyond that, can take on subjective coloring in every respect. This art of speaking can be full of inner warmth which grants access, as it were, to the inner world of the subject and lets us feel his warmth. It was as if that block of ice, the ancient Greek, the *musikē* with its sphinxlike, unapproachable character, now began to break up. Now it gradually began to flow as though transforming itself into a warm stream.

What became of the ancient Greek verse? We have seen how rhythm and verse originated in the time of *musikē*. The word itself was fixed and therefore also language and verse. There was no sharp distinction between verse and music, nor between verse and daily language. Verse was different from daily language only in that certain successions of longs and shorts had crystallized. For some reason certain regular sequences or certain rhythmic patterns were preferred, such as the patterns of our chorus, ∪ ∪ — or — ∪ —. They could have originated also through cult as exclamations or sayings, as, for example, the exclamation ō tŏn ădōnīn, whose rhythm therefore is termed "Adoneus." They were often repeated and thereby became familiar to the Greeks. Thus each verse, each rhythmic pattern, had its particular history, its particular character, its particular application; each formed its own species. There was no basic difference between daily language and verse. There could not be because the language, too, was a fixed physical body.

We have seen that the individual

syllables began to be treated with greater rhythmic freedom even in the time of Plato. Through the progressive dissolution of the fixed character of the rhythm, Greek verse completely lost its original *gestalt* in later times and was transformed into a sentence merely spoken. Since one could no longer distinguish objectively between longs and shorts, a new manner of speaking automatically evolved, and the syllables, as regards objective duration, became neutral and vague. They gave the impression of being all equally short. Duration now depended upon speaking, upon the subject. If we speak a number of such neutral syllables in succession we begin to feel the need for differentiation, for grouping, and automatically the need for *accentuation* is felt.

During the reign of *musikē,* Greek was devoid of accentuation as we know it in modern languages. In Greek one syllable

in every word was particularly prominent, not through accentuation, to be sure,
but rather through melodic emphasis,
perhaps through short melodic ornamentation. This syllable within the word,
however, had nothing whatever to do
with the word's fixed rhythmic structure.
This melodic emphasis, for instance, did
not necessarily coincide with the long.
For example:

$$\overline{} \; \overline{} \; \breve{}\breve{} \overline{} \; \breve{}\breve{} \; \overline{} \; \overline{} \; \overline{} \; \breve{}\breve{} \overline{} \; \breve{}\breve{} \; \overline{}$$
τον παρθενιοις υπο τ' απ'λατοις οφιων κεφαλαις

Here the melodically emphasized syllables are indicated (` , ´ , ˜). If this
line is not realized in the sense of *musikē*,
but is spoken in our modern sense, the
syllables suddenly obtain a special significance and move into the foreground. The
former innocuous, melodic ornamentation
within the word is transformed into that
syllable on which the speaking of the
word is centered. It is transformed into

a dynamic accent. These accents, however, are distributed fortuitously. If, in speaking the line, one is governed by them, an irregular succession of accented and unaccented syllables obtains which has nothing whatever in common with the ancient rhythm:

$$— \; — \; — \; \smile\smile \; — \; \smile\smile \quad\quad — \; — \; — \; \smile\smile \; — \; \smile\smile \; —$$
τον παρϑενίοις ὑπο τ᾽ ἀπ᾽λατοις ὀφιων κεφαλαις

A prose originates, something similar to that resulting from the transformation of the nonpoetic, everyday Greek language. Its distinguishing feature is the free, unregulated succession of accented and unaccented syllables. Prose in the strict sense of the word only now comes into being. This new prose, however, if verse is to originate, suggests the application of a *law* according to which the accents must be ordered: the principle of accentuation demands, as soon as it is accepted as a rhythmic principle of order, a law of the recurrence of accents at equal intervals. Western verse, as we have come to know it, originated in this manner. In other words, the presupposition for a basic separation of prose and verse, for the formation of the antithesis of prose contra verse, is the dissolution of the corporeal, fixed aspect of the language, the abolition of the objective differentiation between the long and the short. In antiquity, particularly in the early period, the artistically formed language could be only *musikē*. Only in western civilization two autonomous possibilities for creation arose: prose, and, derived from it, verse:

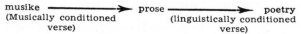

musike   ⟶   prose   ⟶   poetry
(Musically conditioned verse)   (linguistically conditioned verse)

This evolution can be proved historically, too. At the beginning of the tradition of the Greek language we encounter verse as *musikē*, the Homeric hexameter; at the beginning of the history of western Christianity we find the new prose. In prose, Christendom was proclaimed, first in Greek and then in Latin, and prose formed the oldest constituent part and foundation of the Christian liturgy. Verse originated on this plane only secondarily and later, and it no longer contained those rhythmic-musical components which had characterized verse as *musikē*.

What became of the *musical* components of *musikē*? After the new language had become autonomous as prose and as poetry, the musical component of the old *musikē* remained; it, too, became autonomous. It developed its own new musical principle, however, with reference to the new principle of language: even the ordering of accentuation through regular intervals, as it manifested itself in the new verse, was not a linguistic phenomenon in the narrow sense of the

126

word, it was an altogether new rhythmic, new intellectual principle. This principle was now to become the foundation also of music. We have seen previously how the principle of *subdivision* became connected with that of regularly recurring accents in music and in this way led to the origin of the measure in modern western music. *Musikē* was replaced with prose and verse; moreover, a separation of western language from western music took place:

$$\text{Musikē} \begin{array}{l} \longrightarrow \text{Prose} \longrightarrow \text{Poetry (Verse)} \\ \longrightarrow \text{Music} \end{array}$$

From this illustration we can again see that it is false to translate *musikē* as music. *Musikē* cannot be translated, and yet the word lives on in its western variation as "music" to this day, it is on every tongue: the etymological identity points to the origin of our music, to the unity of antiquity and western civilization and to the intellectual continuity from Homer to our time; but the change in meaning points to the powerful, separating factors.

IX

OMETHING REMARKABLE seems to have taken place on Greek soil. We have seen how the Greek language was transformed, a process completed long before Gospel prose came into being. Thus modern Greek originated, yet the ancient rhythm inherent in *musikē* seems to have been so deeply engraved on the human soul that it was able to survive in its own right even after the unity, *musikē*, had disintegrated. When the ancient, solid body of old Greek, of *musikē,* shrank and transformed itself into western language, it left behind a husk, which began to lead its own life, as it were, and became "music" and purely musical rhythm, independent of language. That is the explanation why a stratum of folk music, built according to the old Greek principle of juxtaposition of longs and shorts, is found in modern Greece. It is scarcely necessary to emphasize the importance of this music for the investigation and reconstruction of the ancient Greek rhythm and *musikē:* in vain does the philologist seek access to the rhythm of Greek verse. He has no possibility of finding it, for he is concerned with "language" only. Proceeding from language, none of the modern ones offer a point of departure which would allow him to obtain a correct picture of ancient Greek verse. To the musician familiar with modern Greek folk music, however, a pathway is suddenly opened to ancient Greek language — access from this area naturally could never have been expected by philologists.

Let us give an example, a special case of greatest importance for the reconstruction of ancient Greek rhythm, the rhythm of the Homeric epos:

The Greek rhythmic theorists tell us that the long can be not only twice as long as the short, but can exhibit also the relation $1\frac{1}{2} : 1$. If one equals the short to a quarter note ($\cup$ = ♩) the long can be either a half note (— = ♩) or a dotted quarter (— = ♩.). These arithmetic proportions are exactly described by the musical theorist Aristoxenos, a pupil of Aristotle. The equation of the long syllable with $1\frac{1}{2}$ for the dactyl was claimed by the old rhythmicians: $\overline{1}_{/2}$ $\overset{\cup}{1}$ $\overset{\cup}{1}$ = ♩. ♩♩ . Not only that: it is also expressly stated

that the verse of Homer, dactylic hexameter, is to be executed in this manner.
Despite these unequivocal statements it
has not been possible to make much
headway until recently, for as long as one
"speaks" the verse such distinctions make
little sense. Philologists in general for
that reason have ceased to investigate the
question. Others have attempted to twist
the statements of Greek writers to suit
their own purposes: the fact that
Greek theorists also mention a shortened
long was taken as an indication that
the duration of the long syllable was
not to be considered exact, that the
proportion of duration between longs and
shorts was only approximate, and that,
finally, there was no strict rhythm and
that the verse was to be recited more like
the spoken word in a modern sense. The
shortened long, therefore, according to
this interpretation would refer to nothing

other than the effacement of the rhythms
in a manner similar to that of prose, even
though this contradicts the exact statements of the theorists. Moreover, the old
rhythmic theorists expressly designate
the rhythms with the long as 1½ (♩.) as
rhythms of the round dance, and the
conjecture that this could mean merely
spoken verse must therefore be rejected.
Nevertheless, the prejudice of modern
philologists was so great that this last
factor was simply disregarded. Under-
standably, those unfamiliar with such
rhythms through their own musical
experience cannot possibly associate
anything sensible with them. A rhythm
that not only contradicts the modern
measure, but whose temporal unit
alternates continually between 1½ and 1,
a rhythm whose very foundation seems to
vacillate, appears indeed to be a rhythmic
absurdity. Therefore even the musicians

of today can make little headway with the statements of the Greek theorists.

The situation is different, however, when one is familiar with such rhythm from actual practice: in modern Greece this rhythm not only exists but is a regular and everyday phenomenon. It is the rhythm of the most popular Greek folk dance even today, of the typical Greek round dance, the *syrtós kalamatianós*. Here we find not only the rhythm as described in detail by the ancient rhythmic theorists, but we find it as the rhythm of the round dance, exactly as the ancients tell us. It is a rhythm which consists of three counts, in which the first is longer by one-half than the second and third: $\overset{1}{}. \; \overset{2}{} \overset{3}{}$. Through the hold on 1, which, nevertheless, still does not constitute a full two-count long and is therefore felt to be somewhat transient, and through the pushing forward toward 2 and 3, a "give and take" characteristic of this rhythm and this dance originates, a play between standing still and pressing forward, a peculiar fluctuation. As one dances this round, one feels the elastic quality of this rhythm, but at the same time the static-loose juxtaposition of the individual temporal units. A "give and take" is expressed also by the succession of steps on a larger scale: several steps forward, then a hesitation and a few steps backward.

The basic motive of the steps corresponds to the three counts: a heavy step on 1 — the thesis — and correspondingly lighter (shorter) ones on 2 and 3 — the arsis. We have described similarly the steps for the chorus of Pindar, taking the round dance as our point of departure. As an example we record a *kalamatianós* melody (such Greek folk dance melodies are, of course, handed down only orally, not in notation).

(Basic rhythm: ♩·♩♩; app. ♩· = M.M. 80 ♩ = M.M. 120)

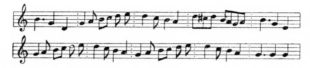

The name of this round dance, *syrtós,* also is important. It is an ancient name for traditional round dances. We find, for instance, the following inscription from Boethia dating from the first century, A. D.: "He devoutly arranged festival processions in the tradition of his fathers and the traditional round dance of the syrtói." *Syrtós* is the only ancient Greek name of a dance which survives in modern Greek folk dances. The representation of round dances in ancient art shows a remarkable resemblance to the picture presented by the modern *syrtói.* Furthermore, one could call to mind the Delian chorus *géranos* and the description of this dance by Homer himself in the 18th song of the *Iliad*.

When all of this is taken into consideration, the striking statement that the concrete and consistent application of this rhythm was claimed by ancient Greek theory for the heroic hexameter, that is, for the rhythm of Homer, takes on immense significance. The rhythm of Homer was just as typical and just as popular in antiquity as the rhythm of the *syrtós kalamatianós* is today. It was the rhythm also of a round dance. The importance of the identity of this modern rhythm with the ancient is even better appreciated when one considers that it is not an ordinary rhythm which, like the 4/4 measure, is encountered every day, but rather one of a most individual and exceptional form.

The modern melodies of the *syrtós* are certainly not as old as its rhythm. They correspond to different stages of history. The rhythm itself, however, is like the original casting mold from which all these melodies have been shaped. It is like a fixed formula, deeply engraved upon the soul of the Greek folk and therefore protected against any caprices of weather and influence of time — in this respect it differs from more labile melodies. The indestructible nature of this rhythm, in the first instance, stems from its relation to the human body as dance; one is tempted, however, to explain it through the original relation of the rhythm to the word, to derive it from the time when this totality was rooted in the soul through the epos. The rhythm was given through the round dance and through the word, it was an unequivocal and immutable *gestalt*. The melodic superstructure, on the other hand, was alterable and not as capable of resistance. We do not believe that one could find a parallel phenomenon in western history, a rhythm which lies outside of the melodic-harmonic development, that is, a rhythm which remained untouched by it.

The two phenomena, the old and the new, the rhythm of Homer and that of the round dance of modern Greece, testify to identical attitudes and have common roots. Here we deal with a similarity founded within, with a relationship anchored in physically experienced movement. Watching this *syrtós kala-matianós,* or taking part in the dancing (in the open air, of course), one feels the ancient tradition in the attitude of the dancers. They exhibit a dignity otherwise foreign to them; their faces become masklike. It is as though an otherwise

139

buried level of consciousness is revealed. In this round dance a force is at work which actually holds the people together and joins them as though under one cupola. The dancers convey a primeval tradition which has been deeply stamped, as it were, upon their very souls; their reverence for their forefathers and their unity with them become manifest. What a concentration of meaning and of vigor this dance must have possessed in the time of its blossoming to persist with such tenacity to this day, to exercise such power over millenia!

Tracing the hexameter to the rhythm of the *kalamatianós* poses the question as to what extent the epos was originally related to dance. This rhythm comes to us today as the rhythm of the round dance, designated as such by the ancients and used for the performance of the Homeric epos. It is indeed possible that the original manner of performance was conceived in relation to the dance, and that it persisted as a popular practice alongside merely recited performances adopted in later centuries. (A remnant of this would be the modern Greek *syrtós kalamatianós*.) Thus we can imagine the dancing of the Phaeaces to the chant of Demodokos in the *Odyssey,* 8th song, in epic hexameter. It would mean that it was possible to sing the epos and at the same time to dance it. At all events, even if the Homeric epos itself was no longer danced, it is clear from what has been discussed that its rhythm, and therewith its connection with the human being in his entirety, originated from the round dance. The one direction of development, the intellectualization of a corporeally bound rhythm into a purely musical or merely recited rhythm of presentation, is a plausible process which is confirmed

141

historically, whereas the reverse procedure is scarcely conceivable. Thus we find in the very beginning of Greek "poetry" — that is, *musikē* — in the time of Homer, and quite possibly even earlier, the impressive unity of music, verse and dance.

This example of the popular modern Greek round dance as the rhythm of Homer clarifies the connection of the history of the ancient with that of the western mind, from Homer to our time, in a particularly beautiful, concrete and striking manner. It illuminates our earlier discussion with reference to the word identity *musikē*-music.

X

Now THAT WE HAVE considered the position of the ancient Greeks we are able better to understand that of western civilization — by contrasting one with the other and thus throwing them into relief, as it were. In *musikē,* as stated earlier, the syllable and the word-body were static, reposing in themselves, existing for themselves. Thereupon a philosophy was based which identified language with the essence of things. The "divine" was embodied in the word as

143

actually present. The substance itself was completely present. We can now add: for the Greeks true "being" was captured in "this world." There was no representation of "another world," one which would weaken true "being," no separation between this world and the next as known to Christianity. With the historical evolution from antiquity to western civilization, however, a change occurred. We have seen that the word-body lost its musical content and that in its place a purely phonetic *gestalt* appeared, conditioned by meaning and dependent upon the speaking subject. The sole element still forming a bridge to musical rhythm was word accentuation, which originated, as we have seen, through the shrinking of the musical word-body. "Filled-in" time evaporated. The accentuation, a principle of unity holding the parts together, separated from the word-body. The same process took place in music. Language and music thereby obtained dynamic character. Substance could no longer be fully present in the word as sound and in the concrete musical rhythm because these phenomena, the sound of the word and musical rhythm, obtained life no longer from within and from their own presence, but rather from an autonomous principle of unity extraneous to them, from the system of accentuation and from the subdivision of measurement. Let us add: the present is not identical with "being," the here and now, for the present is not sufficiently static and has a shadowy quality. Always included in "being" are both past and future. In such language, such music, such intellectual sphere, this world cannot be self-sufficient, because it is too pallid for that. It must relate itself to another world, and through that other world it must justify itself.

The statement that the principle of unity detached itself as a system of accentuation touches upon the objective issue. From a subjective point of view, however, it reveals the following aspect: the principle of unity lies in the *act* of speaking and in the *act* of making music, respectively. This act, therefore, is something dynamic. It obtains this dynamic characteristic, too, in that it can be nothing more than a striving, a longing for "being" and a reference thereto. Related to this process is the new inner warmth of the language and of the music, of which we have previously spoken. Only the prose of western civilization could realize the intellectual position of a St. Augustine: the philosophical and psychological discovery of the individual and of the inner world. A parallel to this development in the language is offered, as we know, by the development from the plastic arts of antiquity to western painting and from the ancient full-bodied, as it were, plastic architecture to the western creation of "interior architecture."

That the word-body evaporated, that *musikē* was transformed into modern prose and divested of its tangible, corporeal quality means that the language, too, became intellectualized, in fact, that it reached the ultimate degree of intellectuality. With it, poetry, too, became something intellectual, even purely intellectual. Poetry no longer represents substance as it did in antiquity. It has become poetry — that is, "art" — in the narrow sense of the word. It must seek its justification elsewhere. Western poetry presupposes a truth proclaimed as prose. Whereas we must think of the origin of *musikē* as from the musical-symbolic word, from musical verse, from song, and must consider prose as its final phase, inversely, at the beginning of western poetry we must see prose as that poetry's original cause and primary source. The straightforward, naive, yet inwardly meaningful prose as a purely intellectual vehicle of meaning reigns over the possibilities of artistic symbolization which it has outgrown. Thereby truth is proclaimed — a purely intellectual understanding, insight, freed from sensuality as the vehicle of art. One can express it this way: whereas *musikē* is sufficient unto itself, is law and fulfillment, religious framework and artistic realization, western poetry presupposes an ultimate religious frame of reference external to itself; it is not conceivable without the simple prose of the *Our Father*. The dependence of western poetry upon prose is not to be understood only from the general intellectual point of view and in connection with the derivation of verse from prose, but pertains to content as well. It is unthinkable to associate the content of the Homeric epos with any sort of prose which might have existed earlier, or to trace it to such prose, whereas in the case of Dante, for example, it is understood that his poetry presupposes not only the prose of the Gospel, but also even that of, say, Thomas Aquinas.

●

In our chorus we have become acquainted with an example of the ancient *musikē*. Let us recall the Epilogue once more, in particular the last line: "unexpectedly time will grant one favor but yet not another." It is, to be sure, impressive even when understood as modern language, as western speech. Let us imagine it as Greek reality, as *musikē:*

$$— \cup — \quad — \quad — \cup \quad — \quad — — \quad \cup \quad — \quad —$$

εμπαλιν γνωμας το μεν δωσει, το δ' ουπω,

How rigidly the words are juxtaposed; how unapproachably absolute is this line, how solid in its inner construction! This pronouncement, masklike in its rigidity, through the static rhythm of "filled-in" time assumes an unalterable quality, something terrifying, and yet precisely because of this quality, an element of liberation. It creates reality itself, and simply by naming it. We can pronounce these words only with awe. Something would be lost if we were to "speak" them meaningfully in the western sense, for that which is present in this Greek line is Fate herself, is deity, and we dare not transform this impact into a pallid human statement.

The Epilogue as a whole (lines 28—32) further presupposes a unity of deity and man which is scarcely understandable to us. It is concerned with Perseus, Athena and the invention of the aulos as much as

it is with Midas, the victor of the contests.
Viewed as a whole, our chorus, our
choréia, must be understood also in this
manner: the myth of the gods, Perseus,
Pythian contests, humans, and Midas
form a unity, a unique reality and
substance. The last line of the strophe
stands by itself, completely self-
sufficient, yet at the same time it
concludes the strophe by rhythmic countermovement, by rhythmic *contrapost.*
The meaning of the rhythmic scheme of
the strophe is fully revealed only in the
last line, not from the content or meaning,
to be sure, but from the fact that the
absolute pronouncement of the last line
and its own rhythm coincide.

How different from this actually
present "being" of our *choréia* is the
behavior of a Christian community in
procession! Here, too, is speaking, singing,
movement, but everything, taken by

itself as here and now, is shadowy and transient, and it makes sense only in relation to another world. The *kyrie eleison* of the crowd in procession is Greek language, to be sure, but it is Christian Greek, a language fundamentally opposed to *musikē*.

"Being" in antiquity differs from "being" in western civilization. Antiquity finds it in this world, western civilization in the separation of this world from the next. However, it would be wrong to ask which of these two outlooks corresponds to true "being." Only one thing can be said: antiquity views it from the aspect of this world, western civilization from that of a contrast between this world and the next. Only the two combined determine our historic-intellectual reality, but who knows what "being" itself — independent of this world and the next — really is? Who knows to what extent "our little life" is of this world *or* the next, of this world *and* the next simultaneously, is probation, illusion or something else unnamed by man, indeterminable by him? Shakespeare has expressed this view in the words, "We are such stuff as dreams are made on, and our little life is rounded with a sleep." Should we read this statement with Christian or with pagan — Greek — accidentals? Either would mean unpermissible restriction. Shakespeare has refrained from interpreting this most profound of all human statements in one way or the other. These words are ancient and Christian at the same time; they embrace antiquity and western civilization, and therein lies their immeasurable greatness. That a human mind was enabled to express this thought became possible only through western-Christian intellectuality, only through the prose of the Gospel.

Metrical Scheme of Pindar's Ode

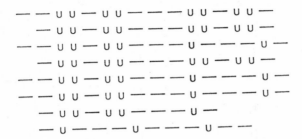

The author also has written a book on this subject in German — not identical with this volume, but quoted for the benefit of those wishing to study the subject further: Georgiades: *Der griechische Rhythmus. Musik, Reigen, Vers und Sprache.* Hamburg, 1949.

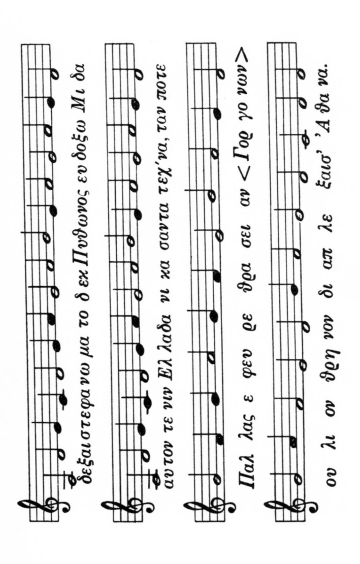